# FABRICATIONS

Work by Kathleen McFarlane

Sainsbury Centre for Visual Arts

University of East Anglia

Norwich

**Fabrications**
Work by Kathleen McFarlane

Sainsbury Centre for Visual Arts
University of East Anglia, Norwich
1 October – 8 December 2002

Exhibition curated by Amanda Geitner and Sara Dutton
Catalogue essays by Veronica Sekules and Linda Theophilus
© the authors 2002
Catalogue and Exhibition Design by George Sexton Associates, Washington, D.C.
Photography by Peter Huggins, Camera Techniques
Photographs of the artist by James McFarlane (pp. 6, 10, 20) and Clare Keegan (p. 23)

Published by the Sainsbury Centre for Visual Arts
University of East Anglia
Norwich NR4 7TJ

ISBN 0 946009 44 9

Printed in Great Britain by Balding + Mansell

The Sainsbury Centre is supported with funds from the

A · H · R · B
arts and humanities research board

Cover:      2. detail *Porifera* 1973
Page 2:     Kathleen McFarlane at Blythe Jex School, Norwich, *c.* 1984
Opposite:   21. *Cycladic Figure* 1984

www.uea.ac.uk/scva
www.katlheenmcfarlane.co.uk

# FABRICATIONS

Work by Kathleen McFarlane

# Contents

Kathleen McFarlane in the garden at Stody, Norfolk, 1971

# Acknowledgements

In recent years, the Sainsbury Centre has initiated and hosted a number of exhibitions in which relationships between materials and form have been both explored and, indeed, pushed to almost subversive limits.

Kathleen McFarlane is an artist who works mainly with textiles and in this, her eightieth year, we are celebrating both a lifetime's artistic achievement and a highly individual and celebratory subversion of both materials and traditional forms which continues to characterise her work. That Kathleen lives and works in Norfolk and has a long association with the University is a happy coincidence… but it has meant that it has been possible for us to have had the great pleasure of working very closely with her on the preparation of the exhibition and its accompanying catalogue.

We are, as always, grateful to those who have lent works; and for this exhibition, particularly, we would like to thank the many people who helped us track down 'lost' pieces from the earlier years of Kathleen's career. Veronica Sekules and Linda Theophilus have contributed fascinating and thought-provoking catalogue essays for which we are immensely grateful, and Kathleen's family have been wonderfully supportive both to the Centre and to Kathleen herself in the preparation of the exhibition.

We invite you to join us in wishing Kathleen a very happy eightieth birthday and in celebrating a vigorous, innovative and forward-looking artist at a particularly creative stage in her long career.

Nichola Johnson
*Director*

**Lenders to the exhibition:**

Amelia Cardoe
David and Shirley Cargill
Professor A.G. and Mrs Margaret Cross
Bill and Helen English
John and Beryl Fletcher
Dr Janet Garton
Valerie Laws
Anne Mackintosh
Alison McFarlane
Andrew and Frances Schumann
Ian Wilson
Lord and Lady Walpole

Aude Gotto, The King of Hearts Gallery, Norwich
Norfolk Museums and Archaeology Service (Norwich Castle)
Suffolk Anglia Polytechnic University, Ipswich
The University of East Anglia, Norwich
Lutterworth Grammar School, Leicestershire
Sudbury Upper School, Suffolk

We would also like to thank those private lenders who wish to remain anonymous.

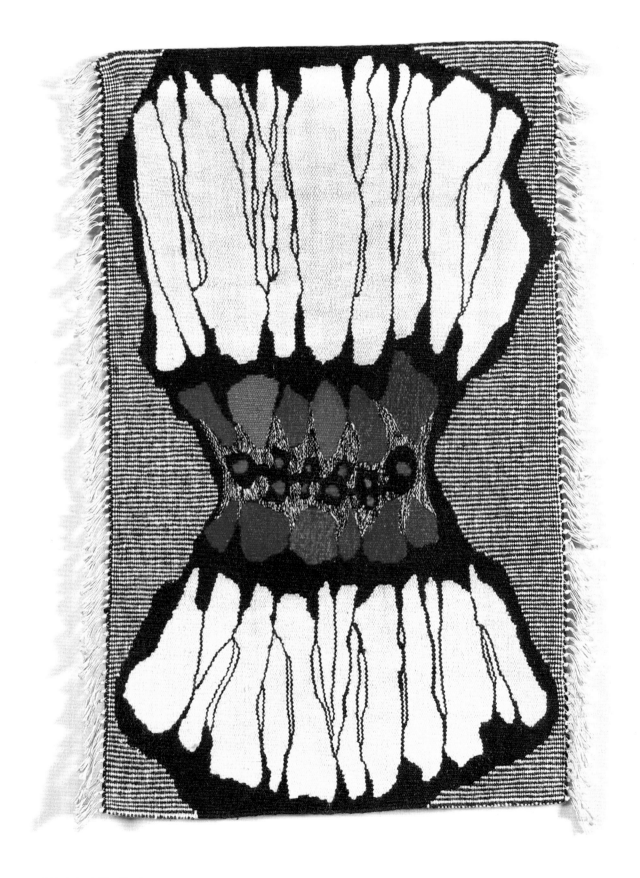

1. *Waisted Radical*   c.1970

# Making Fabrications

Amanda Geitner & Sara Dutton, SCVA

In 2001 we set out to curate a retrospective exhibition in celebration of McFarlane's eightieth year. It was intended that the show focus on the last thirty years of her work. The usually straightforward exhibition process of work selection and loan requests became, in this case, somewhat of a quest. It became a hunt for the many works that had not been seen since they left her house in Norfolk decades ago, but that we had seen pictured in slides taken in Kathleen's studio or garden. Many of the works that we initially uncovered belong to the private collections of individuals who have known Kathleen for many years. We were struck by the enormous affection and attachment that so many people have for the work they live with everyday. Lovingly cared for in their homes, these works have remained in excellent condition and now form the backbone of this exhibition.

Throughout her career, McFarlane has constantly and prolifically produced textile sculptures, flat tapestries, drawings and paintings. The distribution of her work internationally traces her and her husband, Professor James McFarlane's professional and personal travels in Norway and the United States. From a range of exhibitions over the years her work has been sold to unknown buyers, and from her studio she has made commissions and occasional sales that are now very difficult to locate. Our search for her work highlighted the challenge of researching a career that has survived and flourished outside of the commercial and public gallery system.

Unfortunately many of the works we sought for the exhibition have been lost. Key works belonging to corporate and institutional collections had been badly damaged by flood or, indeed, disposed of. McFarlane is regarded as an influential artist in her field and so it was shocking to discover that much work in textile continues to be regarded as soft furnishings, as opposed to fine art, and thus can be removed with a change of management or interior design scheme.

From the start we were captivated by the images of Kathleen's work that we saw in her studio. These images communicated not only the extremely rich variety of her work but also the way in which her techniques and designs had developed over time. **Fabrications** aims to represent the diversity of forms which the artist has pursued and many of those works considered to be her most accomplished and successful are included in the exhibition. Rather than presenting a comprehensive, chronological progression of work, it is by representing this diversity that **Fabrications** becomes a retrospective. A twenty metre work, *Cascade* (cat 40), made by McFarlane in 2002 specifically for the sweeping curved corridor leading to the gallery, brings the range of work in the exhibition to the present day.

Those unobtainable or lost works are represented through images in a gallery slide installation. Of those works which were found, we were all, and no-one more so than Kathleen, surprised at the changes which had occurred in some of the pieces over time. From their inception as pale and cool, the undyed sisal works have become, through everyday exposure to daylight, a warm, deep caramel colour. Others have faded where the tips of the fibres are exposed to light, resulting in a colour gradation that gives the work the luxury and depth of fur.

**Fabrications** has developed from many years of association between Kathleen McFarlane and both the University of East Anglia and the Sainsbury Centre for Visual Arts. Kathleen has an intimate knowledge of the Robert and Lisa Sainsbury Collection and has watched the Sainsbury Centre programme evolve and grow since the opening of the building on campus some twenty-five years ago. In recent years a number of projects, including a Window Show and a flat tapestry commission for the Elizabeth Fry Building, and most significantly the artist's gift, in memory of her husband, of the spectacular *Academic Procession* 2001 (cat 35) tapestry which now adorns the newly refurbished University Council Chamber, have enabled the current staff to work closely with the artist. We are delighted that Kathleen McFarlane's work has found its natural home in the Lower Gallery, in an exhibition that is the culmination of many years of contact and collaboration between the artist and the SCVA.

Kathleen McFarlane in the studio, Stody, Norfolk, *c.* 1975

## Artist's Statement
Kathleen McFarlane

I am conscious of three powerful convictions at work in my tapestries.  Firstly, like any other work of art, a tapestry must express something, communicate something about life and its organic beauty, its magic, its mystery: if ever it starts to become merely decorative, for me it has failed.  Secondly, it must embody a truth to its materials, achieve a sense of rightness, of inevitability almost, so that it captures in itself something of the very nature of growth and life.  Thirdly, like so much of nature, it must hint at the menace that lurks in all beauty, at the terror of innocence.

My implements are wholly traditional: loom, needle and crochet hook.  My materials basic: string, cotton, rope and wool.  My techniques, elemental.  Yet it is the very ordinariness of these things, their utter lack of sophistication, which somehow combine and fuse to form primitive and powerful images.  Indeed the forms take shape in my hands as though they were obeying an inner law, as though demanding to be wholly at one with their medium.  To anyone who is deeply concerned with organic forms as I am, the appeal of this is overwhelming:  it is the challenge of something which is both primitive and at the same time complex, elemental and yet hybrid, traditional and yet uninhibitedly experimental.

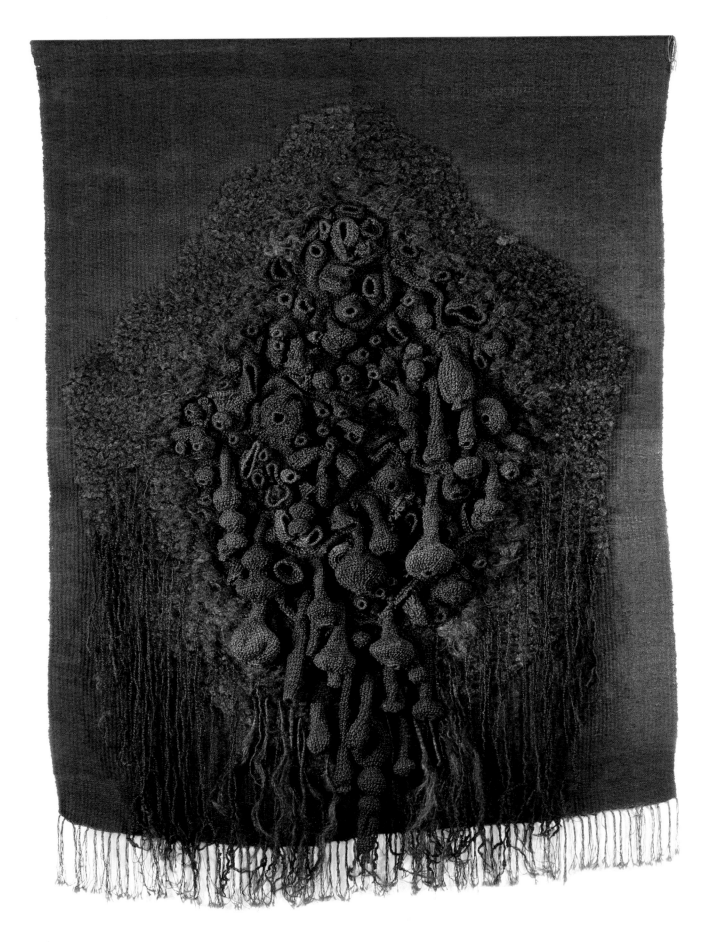

2. *Porifera* 1973
detail *Porifera* 1973

3. *Baboon*  1974
detail *Baboon*  1974

4. *Toreador* 1976
detail *Toreador* 1976

# Fabrications and Contrasts
Veronica Sekules

About fabric, concerned with making, conjuring with substance, truth and illusion. All these elements are present in the title that Kathleen McFarlane chose for her exhibition. But suggestive as it is of materiality and immateriality, it conveys little of her work's substance, drama and physical force.

Kathleen once remarked that cloth forms the first substantial human experience after birth. For a tiny baby, to be enveloped in soft swaddling material must be both comforting and warm and strangely dry and unfamiliar. We are born to a sensual understanding of these contrasting qualities, both pleasurable and fearful, and this is one of the artist's principal reference points. Her tapestries and fibre-works are intensely physical. Most apparent in the three-dimensional reliefs and hangings, there are visceral qualities that come from the fabrication of effects and contrasts, the use of forms that loop, curl, protrude, turn inwardly, droop or spring outwards. Furred wings suggest enveloping warmth; dangling pendants are evocative of bursting spores or dripping fluids. In its directness, its use of familiar, even domestic skills, we think we can understand the crafting and recognize the forms. But here lies another of her fabrications, for the artist's work spars between the maker and the viewer's experience, balancing qualities of attraction and repulsion. It is both enigmatic and absolutely familiar. Its shapes, forms, colours, images can be satisfyingly nestled together, jostling for space and attention; or alternatively, can be, and can make one feel, unaccountably uncomfortable.

Kathleen McFarlane's artistic repertoire is itself a distillation of wide-ranging experience and interests. From a foundation in the Bauhaus-inspired ideas of Victor Pasmore and Richard Hamilton's basic course at Newcastle, with which she had a working familiarity, she developed one strand of her work in abstract painting. It was, in fact, as a painter that her artistic inner life began, at first covertly and unofficially, inspired by, but overshadowed by the professionals. At one time she felt self-conscious about her lack of formal art school qualifications. Increasingly she came to realize that this meant that while she may have lacked a peer group, she gained individuality, strength of purpose and the lack of 'ideological baggage'. Like many artists who are largely self-taught, she has always been driven by strong motivation and inner resources. Her painting continued alongside her growing interests as a weaver and has enabled her to experiment with colour. Indeed, during a period of residence in America in 1984, while her husband James McFarlane (known by all as Mac) was a visiting Professor of Scandinavian literature, she reacquainted herself with the fringes of art school life with a course on colour theory, which spurred her on to new developments both in painting and tapestry.

She came to weaving as a quasi-domestic craft in Newcastle and more or less simultaneously in Norway, where such was the survival of weaving as a craft tradition that peasant households still kept the loom in the living room ready to make all the domestic necessities from bedlinen to rugs, clothing to tablecloths. Coinciding with their move to Norwich in 1964, where Mac took the first chair in European Studies at UEA, came Kathleen's decision to give up translating Norwegian texts and instead combine weaving with looking after their family and household. In traditional Norwegian style, she too kept her magnificent antique Scandinavian loom in the living room; large brown-hued rugs began to fill their home. But it was with the new tapestry and fibre arts emerging from Polish and American artists that Kathleen found the inspiration which eventually allowed her to express ideas in combination with the creation of form. From Magdalena Abakanowicz, the Polish sculptor-weaver whose work in sisal was regularly shown in the Lausanne Tapestry Biennale, and elsewhere in Europe in the early 1960s, she learned that tapestry could be an exciting three-dimensional form in which "anything was possible" (Harrod 1999, 302-3; Waller 1979, 84-9). As Janis Jefferies, who became her pupil, noted, Abakanowicz was an artist who used textile media "to articulate the powerful memories of childhood, of forests and strange spirits, a remembrance of things past that would haunt an increasingly technological world...." (Jefferies 1985, 22-3). For Kathleen this was the revelation she needed. She also became personally

6. *Jacob Sheep* 1977

acquainted with another Polish artist, Tadek Beutlich, the leading figure of British avant-garde tapestry, and from whose book, *The Technique of Woven Tapestry* (Beutlich 1967), she learnt new skills. Kathleen's works from this time were still hybrid forms, between flat tapestry, painting and sculpture, but increasingly experimental. *Waisted Radical* c. 1970 (cat 1), a flat-woven tapestry, part of a series of works in which she bridged two media, shows her emergent interest in the use of imagery from nature to express emotional force, for which her three-dimensional woven sculptures were to give such power as her work matured.

## Craft politics

By 1970, in order to accommodate Kathleen's expanding studio, the family moved to the North Norfolk countryside. Her three children were by now more independent and here was a perfect haven for an artist working in isolation, where she could concentrate on developing and yet still run the household.

By 1973 she showed two major pieces at *The Craftsman's Art* at the Victoria and Albert Museum, an exhibition organised by the newly formed Crafts Advisory Committee, to reflect examples of modern craft works which showed independence of spirit (Harrod 1999, 384). It was a prominent acknowledgement of a new kind of expressive creativity in the crafts which was by now quite well established. Participation in this exhibition brought Kathleen into the metropolitan mainstream and launched the political battle for which she has fought throughout her career: that of status and recognition for the contemporary textile arts, one which, despite a brief period of prominence throughout the 1970s and 1980s, still remains unresolved (Dormer 1997, 174).

One of the works from *The Craftsman's Art*, *Porifera* 1973 (cat 2), was purchased by the Castle Museum in Norwich and was for many years on display in the entrance foyer. Though she was to make several versions in different colours, this dark, brooding work in rich purple-black is the most powerful. She has used the material to give her forms a suggestion of organic growth; the work exists almost as a living thing. Tuboid, cup-like seed-head forms are thickly clustered across the centre. These forms, which became characteristic 'signature' shapes, hover between vegetable and human matter, and appear to be scarcely contained, semi-controlled, bursting. They conjure up nasty associations. Even though we know they are made of dry sisal, the mind invents the dripping, rank slime which escapes from the edges and might at any time be oozing forth some more. *Baboon* 1974 (cat 3) and *Toreador* 1976 (cat 4), from the same period, are, as their names suggest, more overtly zoomorphic. These large images, stretched out like giant pelts of flayed animals, are somewhere between life and death, or perhaps we can see the outstretched wings of a sleeping bat. From the central body dangle more flesh-like protruberances, these seed-pod shapes once more. The cloak-like forms have been compared with the labial forms of Abakanowicz's 'Abakan' tapestries of the mid 1970s (Waller 1976; Harrod 1999, 303), but these are richer in incident: their bodily-sexual allusions, though unintended, are, or appear to be, more explicit. The artist has spoken of her ideas being generated spontaneously as she works on her sculptural tapestries, they are never fully worked out beforehand and inevitably as they take shape, they evoke a number of strands of thought. Her ideas do range across nature of all kinds, though she claims that the explicit sexuality which viewers often remark upon is fortuitous and not something she ever intended to explore. Her husband, Mac's distilled phrases, written for her in the mid 1970s talk of "the menace that lurks in all beauty". Contradiction and conflict is endemic in her works, they are not literalist, and although they deal in visual metaphor they are not linked in any explicit or overt way to particular issues. They remain open to yet further interpretations and conflicts as they are viewed.

In 1973 Kathleen had her first solo exhibition at the Weaver's Workshop in Edinburgh and three years later, at the British Craft Centre in London. For the next five years she was one of the most prominent of the new generation of textile artists working in Britain, her work in demand both for numerous exhibitions and for commissions by private patrons and institutions, from the church, to schools and businesses. Meeting her later, as I did, in 1980, when her career as an artist had reached maturity, she was always extrovert, dressed in vibrant colours and knowing everybody;

Above:    Kathleen McFarlane with *Black Tang*, Stody, Norfolk, *c.* 1975.

working a room with a commanding confidence. It was hard for me to understand that she was of the generation who were expected to stay at home, and as she put it 'sew a fine seam'. Although her home life seemed unutterably happy and her husband unfailingly supportive, she was driven by her own convictions that she had something important beyond that to contribute, to use her work as an escape, as a means of establishing an independent identity.

The 1970s was also the era of the establishment of Feminism, apparently the perfect vehicle for her in this struggle. But, although her work and career epitomised many things that feminists fought for, she was not a joiner, not an ideologist. The kind of causes around gendered skills that feminists espoused in print and artwork: embroidery, knitting, quilting, banners, were just those against which she herself rebelled (Parker 1984; King 1992, 16). And yet, it is inconceivable that her career would have taken the same empowered turn without Feminism. Much of her work is determinedly about women and people were ready to listen to women: indeed younger feminist artists were ready to sit at her feet and learn (Jefferies 1985). A female artist, drawing from her own life and experience, using womens' skills forcefully to her own ends had a new authority and relevance from which she undoubtedly benefited. In a sense also, Feminism has so far failed her in that the status of her craft has hardly changed. Despite the politics (and the involvement of some men, notably Beutlich and Peter Collingwood as artists in the medium), she is convinced that the entrenched notion of textiles as domestic art of little commercial value kept it in the background. If one takes the long view, or the world view, that there is, and has been, no distinction between art and craft, it is entirely a Western categorisation. In *The Art of the Maker,* Peter Dormer argued persuasively for the commonalities of skill across all art forms and media, from painting to calligraphy; that the interdependence of intention and process was a unifying characteristic. An artist in any medium must master its craft sufficiently in order to be able to manipulate it to express ideas, and enable them to develop and progress (Dormer 1994, 70-86). Some years later, bemoaning the fact that artists in textile had little chance to show their work in serious art gallery exhibitions, Dormer returned to the notion of institutionalised prejudice, attributing the lack of mainstream artworld acceptance of the textile arts to the fact that it is differentiated from other art forms by "the use of craft as a medium for creating meaning". This has, on the one hand, emboldened it and "is one of the features that accounts for some of the art textiles energy", but on the other hand, set its own limits, made it inaccessible and specialised. Rather than this being a cause for celebration and discussion, it has caused it to be bypassed: "their *craft* argument is absent. This absence is intellectually perverse but it remains real" (Dormer 1997, 174-175).

Dormer's later polemic was written eighteen years after the foundation of the British 'Fibre Art' movement by Kathleen McFarlane, Miriam Gilbey, Audrey Walker, Janis Jefferies and others. Sitting around after a meeting at Goldsmiths College in London in 1979, then with a growing reputation as a centre for the most exciting emergent textile artists, they decided to promote the new sculptural textiles precisely because they empowered a craft medium and allowed a new means for expressing artistic ideas which needed the status of a movement in line with international developments. Kathleen was the first chair and Janis Jefferies the secretary. Janis has written of this time, with the first Fibre Art exhibition at the Roundhouse in 1980, as one of great inspiration, when, despite Dormer's and other writers' pessimism, they were at a pivotal moment of change (Jefferies 1985). The Fibre Art exhibiting era continued, and one might say culminated, with an exhibition in the following year, *Contemporary British Tapestry*, which Kathleen curated for the Sainsbury Centre (SCVA 1981). It was intended to be a retrospective, reflecting the energy of all the different strands of on and off-loom weaving which constituted the Fibre Art movement. It had wide circulation, touring to Walsall, St Andrews, Edinburgh and Liverpool.

## Nature and Primitivism

Spiky forms of miniature cactus, animal skulls and bones, deformed and twisted roots (*Waisted Radical* c.1970 cat 1), seed pods, patterns in the sand, natural incisions in slabs of stone, delicate winged porcelain pots, elongated Etruscan figurines, swirls of wood grain, strange forms of conch shells… these are some of the objects and photographs that are freely distributed, rearranged and grouped for orderly display in Kathleen's studio and home. An inveterate observer of nature, and collector of small and interesting objects on her travels, she is constantly on the lookout for new sources of inspiration from among a myriad of natural and crafted materials and forms. She is passionate about truth to materials, so as natural forms are transmuted in her work, it is always in a 'weaverly' way, not in a way imitative of the original. She used the fully three-dimensional hangings to transmit a sense of the direct experience of features of the natural landscape, while also being completely part of textile culture. *Hanging Form* 1979 (cat 10) might be a bursting fruit body, but it is also naturally rounded, puffed out and soft-looking. In distilled, adapted, transformed, clouded guise, forms from nature reoccur in her work to express a new language, which is indeed, in Dormer's terms, about and of her craft, but challenges us to define a response which does not yet clearly exist. Her art is truly one of metamorphosis, transforming ideas from one substance to another. The spiral form, found in nature from shells to flowers, appears, distressed, on a large scale in the embryo series. *Black Embryo* 1979 (cat 8), (chosen, as were all her titles after the making) has an ugly beauty, which if one probes too hard may invoke depressing associations, its sombre private folds culminating in strange tails of some indefinable creature. Like a conjurer, the artist changes the mood entirely in its white version, *Embryo* 1981 (cat 15), which is immediately more comforting, like a baby woolly sheep nestling at the centre of a tufted rug. Both these works exploit their craft knowingly to play on the properties of colour and form. In doing so, they invite these kinds of cultural associations with darkness, mystery, fear and comfort, warmth and empathy.

Quite different spiral forms also occur at the centre of *Untitled* 1981 (cat 17). Overall, although this piece is reminiscent of the batwing form of *Baboon* 1974 (cat 3), it is layered differently as if it is a composite of many forms of life. From a distance the central form could be reminiscent of an insect body, it may be an Asmat mask from New Guinea. On closer inspection, it has inevitable allusions to both female and male sexual organs. The upward movement and the springy turf-like texture of its surrounding layer give it, unlike *Baboon*, a life-like context, enhanced by the open, upward-turning slightly rippled wings. The rich associations of this piece, and others in the same family, like *Grey Mask* 1979 (cat 9) owe as much as anything to the art from around the world which the artist saw in the Robert and Lisa Sainsbury Collection, following the opening of the Sainsbury Centre in 1978. Kathleen has described herself as a natural primitive and here at last she found a silent community of like minds, creating art, often from humble materials and basic techniques, making use, just as she had, of their surrounding landscapes and local experience. Never a copyist, she continued to transform. Where she might easily have found textile-rich examples in the Collections, weaving in seagrass or raffia cloth, instead she chose stone. Among her initial sources of inspiration were the pure forms of Cycladic marble figurines to which she made simple neutral tributes, *Goddess* 1976 (cat 5) and *Cycladic Figure* 1984 (cat 21). Both figures use her signature hybrid organic forms, a suggestion of the tightly closed legs and tipped back head of the originals only discernible if you know them. Like many artists who use art collections as a quarry for ideas, the original intentions of the artists she admired were of secondary interest. If they enabled her to bring a new quality of stillness to her work, then she would try to capture some of that spirit. But it was transmitted through the filter of her experience, not theirs.

## Colour and Requiem

The year 1984 saw a temporary move to Madison, Wisconsin and an inevitable change of direction. The move was timely as the heat quickly went out of the Fibre Art movement and already before the trip, demand for heavily worked object-based art was waning. On her return, fresh from her course in colour theory, she brought colour to some of her themes, in strikingly bright hues of purples, pinks and oranges, all of them echoed in the autumn forest landscape. Colour is something which Kathleen has always found hardest of all. She likes colour to assault the viewer, to be confrontational, striking, introducing drama, opposites. She plays with discordant harmonies, strong contrasts and challenging juxtapositions of tones: turquoise and green, reds and blues, black and white, violet and lime. Her most important development following America was a return to flat tapestry. *Magic Carpet* 1986 (cat 24) was woven, without a preparatory cartoon, directly on the loom in her habitual intuitive way, growing organically to

Left:      21. *Cycladic Figure* 1984
Right:    Female Figure with Folded Arms, Early Cycladic *c.* 2700-2400 BC
              Robert and Lisa Sainsbury Collection, UEA
Opposite:  Kathleen McFarlane in her studio with UEA Tapestry on loom, 1994

form a rich, aptly named colour landscape. But around that time also, guided initially by Mac who had been something of a pioneer in computer publishing, she began to experiment with designing tapestry by computer and this helped her resolve problems with colour.

By 1994, the time of her commission on behalf of UEA by Richard Brearley of John Miller and Partners, the architects of the new Elizabeth Fry Building, she was adept and able to produce a host of possible designs on the computer. From these she made four maquettes, after which the final version was chosen and then scaled up. It is a rare architect who will admit that a building can be enhanced by woven textiles, but if ever an argument was needed for the use of tapestry to add character to a space, then this work provides it. Without it, it is still a marvellously light space, dramatically traversed by a glass staircase. But without being at all domineering, the tapestry provides it with a focal point, drawing the eye upwards, adding warmth and life and colour. Four years later, Kathleen made a third tapestry for UEA, a greatly enlarged version of a tapestry of the *Academic Procession* 2001 (cat 35), originally commissioned by her husband. It is now sited permanently in the University Council Chamber.

Mac had always been Kathleen's greatest supporter. Never one to overshadow her, or stand in the way of her development, he admired her work, and gave her the means and the independence to pursue it. His death in 1999 was a terrible blow. But with characteristic resourcefulness, Kathleen allowed her work to take her over the worst times. Having to prepare soon after his death for an exhibition at the King of Hearts in Norwich, she started experimenting with an entirely new series of works in perspex and black and white man-made fibre. Five pieces emerged and almost inadvertently she realised that she had created images of a life cycle: a double helix, sperm, an embryo, the menopause and death. It became her requiem tribute for Mac.

A trip to the Orkney Isles in the year following Mac's death confirmed long-held interests both in prehistory and in sealife. Reflecting her memories of the Orkney coastline, Brochs and Standing Stones, she experimented with *Archaeological Work* 1998 (cat 32), made plaster reliefs impressed with geometric traces. The latest works pursue themes arising from a passionate interest in sea and sea creatures, through continued experimentation with industrial materials, perspex and nylon ropes, which give them quite a new reflective, hard, glittering presence (cats 34, 36). As in her earliest work relating to *Waisted Radical c.* 1970 (cat 1) colour is limited to black, white and red. Only the titles belie the sources of inspiration whether they are from jellyfish, sea anemones, rockpools or shells. The best of the works have the same powerful hybrid qualities as her sisal reliefs, of a new kind of semi-organism and an inventive kind of sculpture, truly craft, but truly art, with the power to attract and repel at the same time.

References
Beutlich, T. (1967) *The Technique of Woven Tapestry*, London: Batsford, New York: Watson Guptili
Dormer, P. (1994) *The Art of the Maker*. London: Thames and Hudson
Dormer, P. (1997) 'Textiles and Technology' in P. Dormer (ed.) *The Culture of Craft*, Manchester University Press
King, C. (1992) 'Making things Mean: cultural representation in objects' in F.Bonner, L.Goldman, R.Allen, L.Jones, C.King (eds.) *Imagining Women*, Cambridge, Polity Press
Harrod, T. (1999) *The Crafts in Britain in the 20th Century*, New Haven, Yale University Press for the Bard Graduate Centre for Studies in the Decorative Arts
Jefferies, J. (1985) 'Material as message', et seq in V. Mitchell (ed.) *Selvedges*, Norwich, Norwich Gallery (2000)
Parker, R. (1984) *The Subversive Stitch. Embroidery and the making of the feminine*, London, Womens' Press
SCVA (1981) *Contemporary British Tapestry* Exhibition Catalogue, Sainsbury Centre for Visual Arts, Norwich
Waller, I. (1976) 'Kathleen McFarlane' in *Crafts* May/June
Waller, I. (1979) *Fine Art Weaving: A study of the work of artist-weavers in Britain*, London, Batsford

8. *Black Embryo* 1979

9. *Grey Mask* 1979

13. *Ram* 1980

12. *Untitled* 1979

17. *Untitled* 1981
detail *Untitled* 1981

14. *Untitled* 1980

16. *White Fungoid* 1981

# A Voyage of Discovery

Linda Theophilus

## Newcastle

Kathleen McFarlane began her artistic career in Newcastle in the 1950s, where her husband James McFarlane (Mac) taught at the University.

*LT: Tell me about those early days....*

*KMcF: I had just lived through a war; I had worked in the Kodak factory in London for four years. I was suddenly thrown into the environment of the academic world; I had had no training in anything, and I didn't rank at all. I had to sink or swim in those conditions. I was part of the intellectual discussion; we were all young and full of ideas about modernism and modern issues. I did my learning where I could find it.*

The McFarlanes' circle included tutors in the University's School of Art: Lawrence Gowing, Richard Hamilton and Victor Pasmore who taught the revolutionary Basic Course with its emphasis on line, form and design. Kathleen became an occasional student at the School and began painting. She was also first exposed to hand weaving via the work of a colleague who made rugs for Heal's.

During this period Mac and she learnt Norwegian together; they worked jointly on translations, and went every year to Norway so that he could continue his study of Scandinavian literature. Kathleen became more interested in the arts and crafts of Norway. She now had two small children and spent her time with neighbouring housewives, where "everyone had a loom in the corner". Here she learnt to weave. Norwegian weaving is based primarily on a folk tradition, using geometric designs, tapestry weave and traditional strong colour combinations (for example, black, white bright gold/brown and mustard).

*KMcF: I brought back a loom from Norway and set it up in the nursery. I couldn't paint but I could weave and watch over small children. I was weaving endless rugs, using carpet 'thrums' (off cuts of wool yarn from the near by carpet factory).*

Examples of these rugs are still in use in her house – striped black, lime, mustard, white and cream – hardwearing and stylish. But by the early 1960s she wanted to move on from making domestic textiles.

*KMcF: It was so vibrant an art scene in that period in the North.... I wanted to make my weaving an art form. I began to make flat tapestries, linked to my paintings.*

*Waisted Radical c.* 1970 (cat 1) is a fine example of these early pieces – it is made using tapestry weave on her horizontal loom. The warp threads are inserted by hand, and do not run from edge to edge, but are woven back and forth, building up small adjacent areas of colour. This method of weaving creates undulating textures, rather than the regular grided surface of a shuttle-made textile. The strong red/black/white palette is augmented with areas of plying (when yarns of different colours are twisted together before being woven) and unstitched slits, which add a black outline, created by the shadows. Traditionally, tapestries are woven on their sides, the weft threads running from top to bottom when the tapestry is hung. This gives an elongated character to the design, which McFarlane has used to great advantage in this piece, translating the rapid, energetic vertical mark making of her paintings of that time into the parallel art form of textile.

16. detail *White Fungoid* 1981

**Norwich**

In 1964 Mac was invited to join the team that set up the then new University of East Anglia. Kathleen continued to weave, but against the pressures of their new life.

*KMcF: In Norwich I had a room where I could set up my loom, and the children were growing up but I threw myself into the life of the University for the first five years – again I was always surrounded by high profile people, coming in and out of the house. I couldn't feel important in that climate; I was an amateur. If I had been to art school I would have thought of myself as a professional. I could have played golf or bridge – but I made art. A passionate question of indulgence on my part – although I was intimidated by all these people, it clearly didn't kill the urge. I never doubted my right to do it or my need to do it.*

*LT: And were you still painting and making flat tapestry at this point?*

*KMcF: Yes – I saw Tadek Beutlich's book (The Technique of Woven Tapestry) in the library in Norwich, and taught myself from that.*

*LT: Did you exhibit and sell your work at this time?*

*KMcF: Oh yes they were bought – I had exhibitions – in Norwich and at the Craft Centre in London (at Hay Hill). As the children grew up, I could start dedicating myself more to my work. I needed to distance myself from University life – I got involved in everything but I wasn't doing enough work. I had continued to work with Mac on Norwegian translations, but now I wanted to be an artist.*

*LT: Internationally this was a very exciting period for textiles wasn't it?*

*KMcF: Oh yes; I saw Tadek Beutlich's work regularly in the Grabowski Gallery in London. And while in Amsterdam, I saw the work of the great Polish artist Magdalena Abakanowicz. They were using sisal and their work was 'off the surface'. It had a huge impact – the scale, the content. And it wasn't about painting. It was textile as a work of art. That's what struck me. I still feel the shock of walking into the Stedelijk and seeing Magdalena's work in the central hall, and thinking "this is the way I have to go." It moved my work into a quite different dimension.*

**Stody**

In 1971, the family moved to Stody, a tiny hamlet some twenty miles north of Norwich. The house sits in a now beautiful garden that slopes up to woods behind and with trees all around. It reminded them of a clearing in the Norwegian forest, and the house "suited our needs" including a separate studio for Kathleen. The elements from which she would build her mature work were all in place – the skills, the time and space, the inspiration of Beutlich and Abakanowicz …and a great impetus to make work, to 'be an artist'.

*LT: You have talked about getting into your stride when you were fifty… re-channelling the creativity of motherhood into a new area…..*

*KMcF: We moved out of Norwich because I felt the University was consuming me. I loved it; I met many interesting people. But I wasn't doing any work. I was forty-nine when we moved here – children had left home, post-menopause and all of that. I think something quite profound has happened in society – it hasn't quite been recognised how liberated women are when the children have left, and they have a whole other lifetime ahead of them to use. I felt forcibly as if I had a lid on me and when I lifted it a great head of steam erupted….and it's gone on erupting!*

*LT: Tell me about your work at this period… you too began using sisal. That has a resistance – it's tough, robust.*

*KMcF: Sisal makes a structure that will hold its shape; you can make sculpture from it. You can't make sculpture of wool – it doesn't have the body.*

LT: And you began using crochet...

KMcF: Magdalena Abakanowicz had one crocheted element on one of the works that I saw – and this must have meant something to me – I knew how to crochet. I started endlessly crocheting.

LT: Tell me more about your way of working in the early 1970s. At first the pieces were rectangular, with areas of deep relief – tufting and elements away from the surface in the central portion...

KMcF: I assembled the crocheted shapes onto a woven background. I was still working on my horizontal loom to make the backgrounds.

LT: Looking at the pieces, one can see that your backgrounds are quite varied, you used different weaves, achieved different effects...(Untitled 1979 cat 12; Embryo 1981 cat 15)

KMcF: The background for White Fungoid 1981 (cat 16)... was just a piece of flat tabby weave with an area of tufting made on the loom. I did vary the weave – but I was making flat pieces that you rolled on.

To increase the scale, the backgrounds were sometimes made in two halves and sewn together. A visit from the Scottish tapestry weaver Archie Brennan proved liberating – he suggested a large scale frame loom, like those used by his weavers at the Dovecot Studios in Edinburgh. This enabled her to work on both sides of the fabric, to include areas of much heavier tufting and texturing and to see the whole piece during the making. The vertical loom, made by Brennan's father still spans the wall of her studio.

KMcF: It was a very big frame – I first made Black Tang. Being who I am I met the challenge and made it the full size of the frame and two sided. I worked back and front – and I think that was the best one I ever made, it was huge.

LT: So that radically changed the way you worked...

KMcF: It was a big change; I started to think in three dimensions. This was such coarse weaving – I was weaving about two or three warps to the inch; I could use whole rope as well. It enabled me to work much faster; I could make half a tapestry in a day.

But working on the vertical frame loom was only one element in achieving the magnificent pieces of the 1970s. In some examples (Embryo cat 15, and Black Embryo cat 8) the central area is formed from a flat woven piece, which Kathleen has manipulated after it is woven, folding and forming it, stitching it onto the background cloth. In Untitled 1981 cat 17, and spectacularly in Bird of Prey 1979, cat 11, and Toreador 1976, cat 4, she has exploited the drape and hang of woven cloth to produce the deep folds, the resting weight, the shadows and highlights of Bird of Prey's 'wings', and to different effect, the loom and billow of the heavily textured 'cloak' in Toreador.

LT: I am interested in the complex nature of these pieces – you are using a variety of techniques –

KMcF: The whole thing is built on my domestic skills – crochet, weaving, stitching, dressmaking. Textiles surround us all our lives – you are born with them, and live with them. Particularly for women. All the years I was raising the children and not making much of my own work, I did all the creative things – I made their clothes, I knitted for them. With my tapestries, I was taking flat pieces of weaving and as you make a dress, fitting them together to form the three-dimensional form I wanted. I didn't have to learn that.

Above: 15. Embryo 1981

35

*The earliest I made like this was huge (Black Tang sold to a hotel chain in America). That was when I started manipulating quite coarse fabric, and discovering these wonderful organic shapes – it almost made itself.*

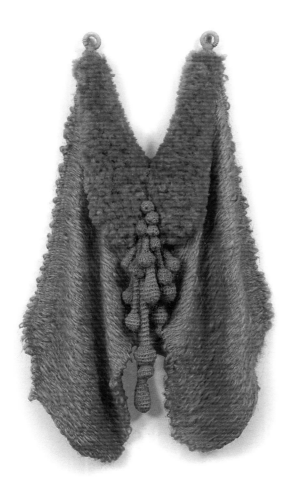

*LT: But tell me about your ideas...the concepts behind the making...*

*KMcF: When I saw the shapes that were growing from crochet, growing out of my hands...I just couldn't believe how significant they were... they had a very profound impact on me.*

*LT: They refer to the statement about your work, written at that time: the menace that lurks in all beauty...the terror of innocence...*

*KMcF: Oh yes it couldn't be pretty...The forms are so inherent in the materials and the techniques. And you feel the menace of it, not quite knowing what will appear. My work is about primitive emotions and primitive ideas. It comes from a different part of the brain. Victor Pasmore would say "Dredge your mind for ideas; get it from the back of the mind, not the front". For me, all this was in Magdalena Abakanowicz's work, and in Jungian influences, which Mac was writing about at that time... all these were part of the ideas that surrounded me. Ideas come earlier into your imagination and you fertilise them – but the selection is yours; you only pursue ideas that you want to follow.*

The achievements of these experimental and energetic years were quickly recognised when the Crafts Advisory Committee (later the Crafts Council) included McFarlane's work in *The Craftsman's Art*, staged at the Victoria and Albert Museum, London in 1973.

*KMcF: I showed two big pieces in the exhibition. At the time, I didn't realise the significance of being included, but this made me a serious artist. After the exhibition, Norwich Castle bought one of the pieces (Porifera 1973 cat 2). It hung in the entrance for thirty odd years. It established my reputation in Norwich.*

### America
In 1983-4, McFarlane spent a year in America, where she made and exhibited a new series of sisal pieces, based this time on the figure – elongated, suspended shapes with rudimentary bellies, heads and features. During the visit she also studied the tapestries of the Navajo and the Mexican Indians, and completed a course in colour theory at the University of Wisconsin.

### Stody
On her return to Norfolk, she began to paint and make flat tapestries again, this time soaked in vibrant colours and influenced by landscape. As with her earlier tapestries they bear the influence of Norwegian 'peasant' tapestry rather than the traditional Gobelin. Her pastel drawings, which she refers to as her 'holiday snaps' are done on site. They are full of rapid strokes and direct observation of the changing light on the rugged hills of her native Northumberland, or the sun-soaked colours of France.

*LT: Your visit to America represented a kind of renaissance for you.*

*KMcF: It was – I had used low key colour in my earlier tapestries. And I had dyed sisal using procion dyes and dustbins as dye baths. I had always felt passionately about colour. After the course in America, I became very interested in pushing colour as far as I could, but it is very difficult.*

Above:    11. *Bird of Prey* 1979

36

LT:  And you have spoken about designing on the computer – like the introduction of the frame loom, the computer also gave a new impetus.

KMcF:  Yes different equipment can take you in a different direction.  Using the computer helped me with the balance of colour which really is hellish difficult – I must have thousands of computer images for designs, because you can do them in seconds.  I also make drawings all the time.  When I can't think of anything else to do, I fill sketch books with black and white doodles.  Somehow, I can't draw like that on the computer.

LT:  Looking at the large tapestry you were commissioned to make for the Elizabeth Fry Building at the University of East Anglia (Untitled 1994 cat 29) and the Maquettes,(cats 26, 27 and 28), it is apparent that the designs were developed both from your work on the computer, and to the chevrons and arrow heads that appear in your black and white sketches.

As well as making tapestries, McFarlane is again experimenting with new materials and techniques.  This time using acrylic plastic sheet and man-made ropes and twines, she manipulates the materials with a hot-air gun, producing curves and flows as the rigid sheet begins to soften and melt.  She teases out the yarn into hair-like fronds, or coils and crochets it into DNA-like spirals.  The pieces are smaller – a body-width across – and again are unsettling images; certainly sexual but also ambiguously sea anemones, plants, organic forms, rugged landscapes.  She has returned to the forms and working methods which have preoccupied her for so long, and which she sums up by repeating lines from the writings of Knut Hamsun, a quotation that has become a personal mantra over the years: "trackless journeying by brain and heart, the whisper of the blood, the entreaty of the bone, all the unconscious life of the mind".

Having worked in relative artistic isolation for much of her career, McFarlane is still eager for discussion about artistic ideas.  With skills honed in the world of academic debate, she is a passionate and entertaining defender of the crafts in the field of fine art.  Her sense of exploration – that head of steam – she identified in 1970, continues to drive her work forward.

KMcF:  I've got to be working all the time.  Currently I am making very rigid forms by crocheting over rope – like a basket – another dimension I have yet to try.  I have to have new challenges all the time.  I feel very passionately that if you push things too far they go dead.  So it is a constant voyage of discovery for me.

Kathleen McFarlane was born in 1922, the same year as two other ground-breaking British based weavers – Peter Collingwood, widely influential through his inventive changes to the loom and his clear and logical analysis of textile structures, and Tadek Beutlich, who so inspired McFarlane in the 1960s.  Along side these, McFarlane's achievement is in marrying a range of domestic textile techniques with a command of weaving and an instinctive and sensual pleasure in materials.  Using this pallette, she achieves in her major works the visceral 'hit', the 'getting beneath' the respectable and the polite that is an important element of good visual art.

Based on a taped conversation between Kathleen McFarlane and Linda Theophilus
Stody, Norfolk, July 2002

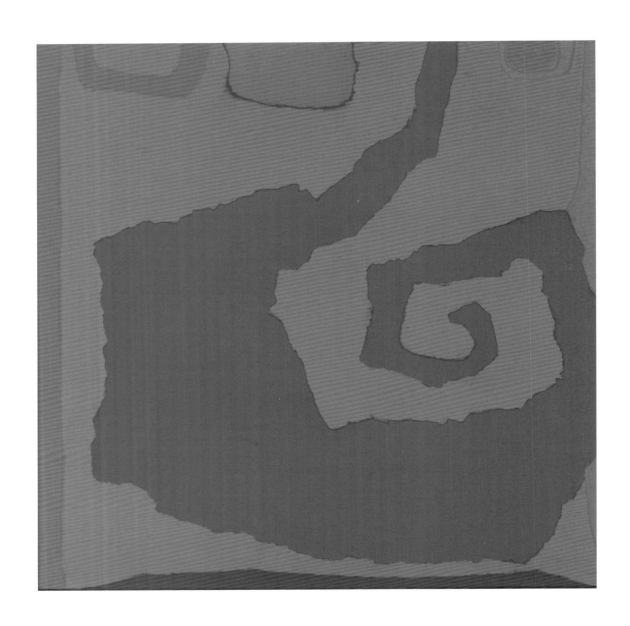

19. *Cyclone* 1984

20. *Image from Prehistory* 1980

22. *Michaelmas* 1985

(following pages)

24. *Magic Carpet* 1986

23. *Easter* 1986

18. *Vulture* 1981

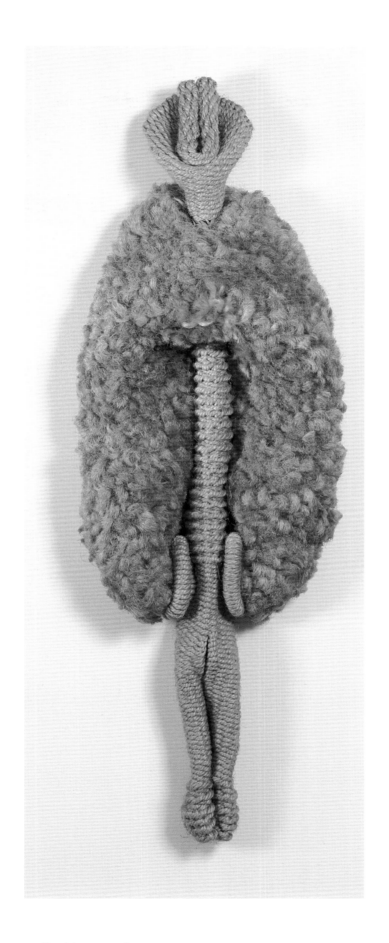

5. *Goddess*  1976

26. *Maquette for UEA Tapestry* 1994

27. *Maquette for UEA Tapestry* 1994

28. *Maquette for UEA Tapestry* 1994

29. *Untitled* (UEA Tapestry)  1994

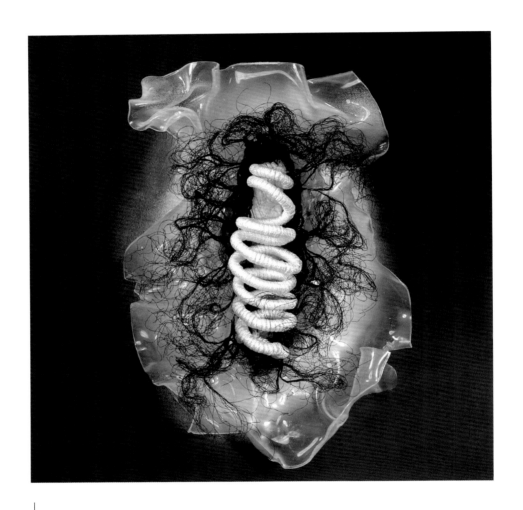

I

33. *Life Cycle I-V* 1999

(preceding pages)

35. *Academic Procession*  2001

I

II

25. *Landscapes I-IV  c.* 1990

III

IV

32. *Archaeological Work I-IV* 1998

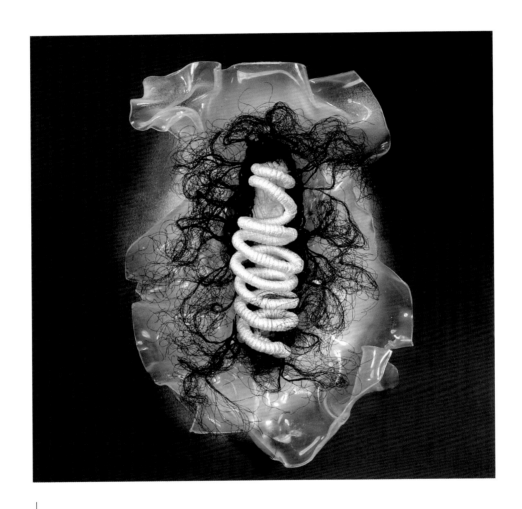

I

33. *Life Cycle I-V* 1999

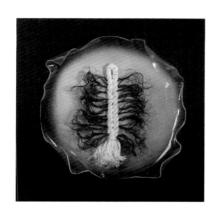

II

III

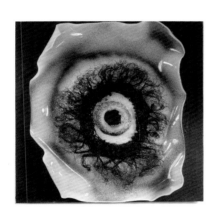

IV

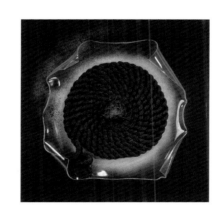

V

# List of Works

1. *Waisted Radical* c. 1970
   Woven wool tapestry
   104 x 61 cm
   From the Collection of
   John and Beryl Fletcher

2. *Porifera* 1973
   Woven, crocheted and knotted sisal
   270 x 200 cm
   Norfolk Museums and Archaeology
   Service (Norwich Castle)
   Presented by Norfolk Contemporary
   Crafts Committee 1974

3. *Baboon* 1974
   Woven and crocheted sisal
   155 x 63 x 5 cm
   Lutterworth Grammar School,
   Leicestershire

4. *Toreador* 1976
   Woven, crocheted and knotted sisal
   310 x 300 cm
   Sudbury Upper School, Suffolk

5. *Goddess* 1976
   Woven and knotted sisal
   145 x 50 x 15 cm
   Courtesy the artist

6. *Jacob Sheep* 1977
   Woven and crocheted sisal
   120 x 100 x 30 cm
   Private Collection
   Courtesy of Lord and Lady Walpole

7. *Interlocking Forms* 1978
   Woven sisal
   100 x 35 x 18 cm
   Suffolk Anglia Polytechnic University,
   Ipswich

8. *Black Embryo* 1979
   Woven sisal
   105 x 78 x 20 cm
   Courtesy the artist

9. *Grey Mask* 1979
   Woven, knotted sisal
   88.5 x 46 x 13 cm
   Courtesy the artist

10. *Hanging Form* 1979
    Crocheted sisal
    135 x 20 x 20 cm
    Private Collection
    Courtesy of Helen and Bill English

11. *Bird of Prey* 1979
    Woven, crocheted and knotted sisal
    164 x 125 cm
    Private Collection
    Courtesy of Anne Mackintosh

12. *Untitled* 1979
    Woven, crocheted and knotted sisal
    140 x 140 cm
    Private Collection
    Courtesy of Amelia Cardoe

13. *Ram* 1980
    Woven sisal
    120 x 60 x 12 cm
    Private Collection
    Courtesy of David and Shirley Cargill

14. *Untitled* 1980
    Woven and knotted sisal
    140 x 90 x 15 cm
    Private Collection

15. *Embryo* 1981
    Woven and knotted sisal
    150 x 110 x 15 cm
    Private Collection

16. *White Fungoid* 1981
    Woven and crocheted sisal
    138 x 100 x 20 cm
    Private Collection courtesy of
    Prof A.G. and Mrs Margaret Cross

17. *Untitled* 1981
    Woven and knotted sisal
    90 x 138 x 24 cm
    Private Collection
    Courtesy of Dr Janet Garton

18. *Vulture* 1981
    Crocheted and knottted sisal
    150 x 140 cm
    University of East Anglia Collection

19. *Cyclone* 1984
    Acrylic on canvas
    73.5 x 73.5 cm
    Courtesy the artist

20. *Image from Prehistory* 1980
    Woven wool tapestry
    103 x 81 cm
    Private collection
    Courtesy of Alison McFarlane

21. *Cycladic Figure* 1984
    Woven and knotted sisal
    145 x 43 x 15 cm
    Courtesy the artist

22. *Michaelmas* 1985
    Woven wool tapestry
    110 x 150 cm
    Courtesy the artist

23. *Easter* 1986
    Woven wool tapestry
    94 x 145 cm
    Courtesy the artist

24. *Magic Carpet* 1986
    Woven wool tapestry
    94 x 128 cm
    Collection of Mrs Aude Gotto,
    The King of Hearts Gallery, Norwich

25. *Landscapes I-IV* c. 1990
    Oil pastel on paper
    I   22 x 19 cm
    II  26 x 29 cm
    III 47 x 40 cm
    IV 49 x 43 cm
    Courtesy the artist

26. *Maquette for UEA Tapestry* 1994
    Woven wool tapestry
    88 x 66 cm
    Private Collection courtesy of
    Andrew and Frances Schumann

27. *Maquette for UEA Tapestry* 1994
    Woven wool tapestry
    85 x 71 cm
    Private Collection

28. *Maquette for UEA Tapestry* 1994
    Woven wool tapestry
    80 x 72 cm
    Private Collection
    Courtesy of Ian Wilson, Bath

29. *Untitled* (UEA Tapestry) 1994
    Woven wool tapestry
    214 x 153 cm
    University of East Anglia Collection

30. *Goddess* (Grizedale series) 1998
    Woven and knotted sisal
    165 x 31 cm
    Courtesy the artist

31. *Scarlet and Blue* 1998
    Crocheted and knotted sisal
    73 x 45 x 15 cm
    Courtesy the artist

32. *Archaeological Work I-V* 1998
    Plaster
    Each 46 x 46 cm
    Courtesy the artist and Valerie Laws

33. *Life Cycle I-V* 1999
    Acrylic sheet and man-made fibre
    Each 46 x 46 cm
    Courtesy the artist

34. *Sea Urchin* 2001
    Acrylic sheet and crocheted
    man-made fibre
    21 x 31 x 31 cm
    Courtesy the artist

35. *Academic Procession* 2001
    Woven wool tapestry
    150 x 334 cm
    University of East Anglia Collection

36. *Sea Creature* 2002
    Crocheted sisal
    190 x 40 x 40 cm
    Courtesy the artist

37. *Phylum with Spiral* 2002
    Crocheted sisal
    190 x 40 x 40 cm
    Courtesy the artist

38. *Jelly Fish* 2002
    Acrylic sheet and textile
    190 x 40 x 40 cm
    Courtesy the artist

39. *Rock Pools I-IV* 2002
    Acrylic sheet and man-made fibre
    Each 31 x 31 cm
    Courtesy the artist

40. *Cascade* 2002
    Woven man-made fibre
    2.5 x 12 metres
    Courtesy the artist

36. *Sea Creature* 2002

57

37. *Phylum with Spiral* 2002
38. *Jelly Fish* 2002

34. *Sea Urchin*  2001

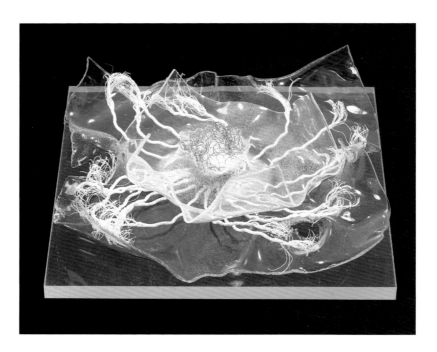

I

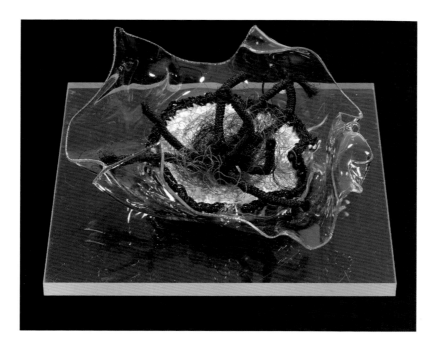

II

39. *Rock Pools I-IV*  2002

III

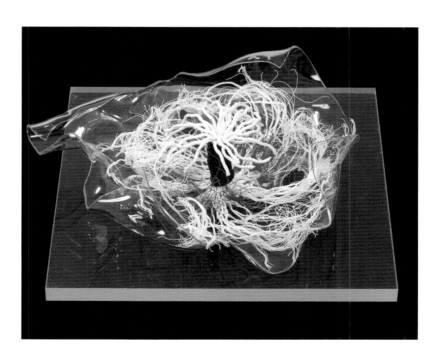

IV

Kathleen McFarlane with *Toreador* 1976 cat 4, in the Lower Gallery, SCVA, 2002

# Biography

Born 1922

## Solo Exhibitions

1973  Weavers' Workshop, Edinburgh
1976  British Crafts Centre, London
1977  Gardner Centre, University of Sussex, Brighton
1980  Wells Arts Centre, Norfolk
1982  The Artist at Work, Castle Museum, Norwich
1984  University of Wisconsin, USA
1995  Advice Arcade Gallery, Norwich
1996  Wingfield Arts, Suffolk
1997  Window Show Sainsbury Centre for Visual Arts, Elizabeth Fry Building, University of East Anglia, Norwich

## Shared Exhibitions

1970  Norwich Triennial festival:
      Elm Hill Craft Shop, Norwich (with Peter Lane)
1974  Sunderland Art Gallery:
      Festival Exhibition, Sunderland (with Wendy Ramshaw)
1976  Norwich Triennial Festival:
      St Andrews Hall, Norwich
      (with Peter Lane and Lorraine Fernie)
1992  King of Hearts Gallery, Norwich
      (with Andrew Schumann)

## Group and Mixed Exhibitions

1973  *The Craftsman's Art* V&A, London
1973  *Fifteen Weavers* British Crafts Centre, London
1974  *British Tapestries and Hangings* Weavers Workshop, Edinburgh
1975  *Woven Works: Eastern Arts* Travelling Exhibition
1975  *Ceramics and Weaving* Kettle's Yard, Cambridge
1975  *Contemporary Weaving* Usher Gallery, Lincoln
1975  Design Centre, London
1976  *Contemporary Tapestries* DLI Gallery, Durham
1976  Design Centre, London
1976  *Woven Hangings* Minories Gallery, Colchester
1977  *Masterpieces* British Crafts Centre, London
1977  *Textiles* British Crafts Centre, London
1978  *Twelve Sculptors* West Surrey College of Art
1979  *British Craftsmen* Bergens Kunstindustrimuseum, Norway
1980  *Craft of the Weaver* (BBC Exhibition) British Crafts Centre, London
1980  *Fibre Art* The Round House Gallery, London
1981  *Contemporary British Tapestry* Sainsbury Centre, Norwich
      also at Walsall Museum and Art Gallery,
      Crawford Centre for the Arts, University of St Andrews
      Talbot Rice Centre, University of Edinburgh
      Bluecoat Gallery, Liverpool
1983  *Textiles as Sculpture* Wells Arts Centre, Norfolk
1996  *Contemporary British Tapestry* Barbican Centre, London
1997  Mannington Hall, Norfolk

## Public and Corporate Collections

Norwich Castle Museum
Leicester Education Authority
Eastern Arts Association
Suffolk Education Authority
Norfolk Education Authority
British Ropes
University of East Anglia

## Bibliography

Chloë Colchester, *The New Textiles: Trends and Traditions*, London: Thames and Hudson, 1991
Miriam Gilbey, *Free Weaving*, London: Pitman, 1986
Xenia Parker, *Creative Handweaving*, New York: The Dial Press, 1976
Ann Sutton, *British Craft Textiles*, London: Collins, 1985
Irene Waller, *Fine Art Weaving*, London: Batsford, 1979

## Also relevant are the following

Crafts Council Index: *Craftsmen of Quality*, London: Crafts Advisory Committee, 1976
Crafts Council, *The Makers*, V&A, 1975
*The Craftsman's Art*, London: Crafts Advisory Committee, 1983
Kathleen McFarlane, *Contemporary British Tapestry*, University of East Anglia, Norwich, 1981

## Also featured in

Crafts Magazine, March/April 2000 *Sources of Inspiration*
BBC TV series *The Craft of the Weaver*
Anglia ITV series *Folio*